BATARANGS AND GRAPNELS

THE SCIENCE BEHIND BATMAN'S UTILITY BELT

BY AGNIESZKA BISKUP

BATMAN CREATED BY
BOB KANE
WITH BILL FINGER

BATMAN SCIENCE

CAPSTONE PRESS
a capstone imprint

Published by Capstone Press in 2014
A Capstone Imprint
1710 Roe Crest Drive
North Mankato, Minnesota 56003
www.capstonepub.com

STAR30538

Library of Congress Cataloging-in-Publication Data
Biskup, Agnieszka.
  Batarangs and grapnels : the science behind Batman's utility belt / by Agnieszka Biskup ; Batman created by Bob Kane.
     pages cm.—(Batman science)
  Includes bibliographical references and index.
  ISBN 978-1-4765-3943-0 (library binding)
  ISBN 978-1-4765-5211-8 (paperback)
1. Batman (Fictitious character)—Juvenile literature. 2. Weapons—Juvenile literature. 3. Tools—Juvenile literature. I. Kane, Bob. II. Title.
  PN6728.B36B635 2014
  700'.451—dc23   2013028327

Summary: Explores the real-world science and engineering connections to the gear in Batman's Utility Belt.

Editorial Credits
Editor: Christopher L. Harbo
Designer: Veronica Scott
Production Specialist: Kathy McColley

Photo Credits
Alamy: Bob Daemmrich Photography/Marjorie Kamys Cotera, 16, louise murray, 28, National Geographic Image Colleciton/Gregory A. Harlin, 12, WaterFrame, 29; DoD photo by Luis Viegas, 22, MCSN Martin Carey, U.S. Navy, 20; Getty Images: AFP/Kazuhiro Nogi, 9; Glow Images: SuperStock/Science Faction, 15; Newscom: imago sportfotodienst, 19; UPI/Kevin Dietsch, 26 (right); Shutterstock: Andrey_Kuzmin, 26 (left), 27, digitalreflections, 13 (bottom), farres, 8, Gavran333, 7, Joe White, 18, Melissa Brandes, 10, PinkBlue, 21, Sergio Schnitzler, 13 (top); U.S. Air Force photo by Tech. Sgt. Jeremy T. Lock, 23; U.S. Army photo by Markus Rauchenberger, 11 (top), Sgt. Pablo N. Piedra, 11 (bottom); U.S. Marine Corps photo by Cpl. David Hernandez, 24; U.S. Navy Photo by John Narewski, 25

Design Elements: Shutterstock: BiterBig, ClickHere, Jason Winter

TABLE OF CONTENTS

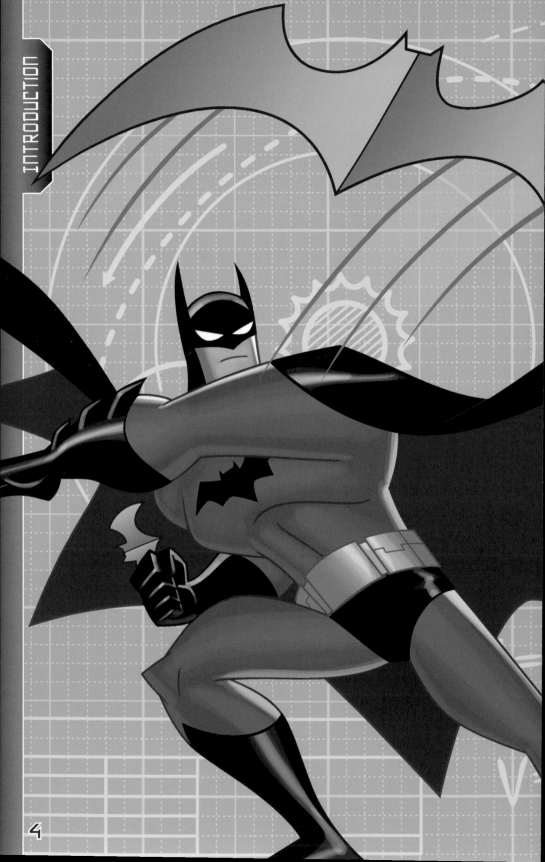

SUPER HERO GADGETS AND GEAR

Almost every super hero has one special tool that defines him or her. Wonder Woman slings her Golden Lasso of Truth. Green Lantern uses a power ring. Aquaman wields his trusty trident. But none of these tools is quite like Batman's Utility Belt.

Designed as the ultimate crime-fighting toolkit, Batman's Utility Belt carries everything he needs. With its gear-attachment system, every gadget Batman carries is within arm's reach. For the Caped Crusader, the Utility Belt can mean the difference between life and death.

While Batman's Utility Belt is cool on its own, its connection to the real world might surprise you. For starters, take a look at real-life crime fighters. Police officers and soldiers wear duty and service belts to hold their equipment. But the connections don't stop there. The gear on Batman's Utility Belt has the most amazing links to the real world. While he fights crime in a fictional world, much of Batman's gear is based in reality.

BATARANGS AND GRAPNEL GUNS

The Batarangs and grapnel gun on Batman's Utility Belt would make any super hero jealous. But you don't have to be a super hero to find their connections to the real world.

BOOMERANG BASICS

When Batman has a criminal on the run, he often reaches for his Batarangs. The Caped Crusader has used these bat-shaped weapons throughout his career. While Batman has several types of Batarangs, some of them work like boomerangs.

Most people picture a boomerang as a curved stick that returns after being thrown. But not all boomerangs come back. In fact, many ancient boomerangs were hunting weapons that didn't return. They were shaped throwing sticks that flew well through the air.

Boomerangs that can return to the thrower are different. They usually have two wings joined in the middle. Set at a slight tilt, these wings allow air to flow over their surfaces. This airflow creates **lift**.

When thrown, a returning boomerang has two kinds of motion—a spinning motion and a forward motion. The spinning motion causes uneven lift on the wings. One wing moves forward in the direction of the flight. The other wing moves backward against the direction of the flight.

While uneven lift tries to tip the boomerang over, the spinning motion twists the tipping forces at right angles. Together these forces give the boomerang its curved flight. It's similar to how leaning on a moving bike makes it turn. Thrown correctly, a boomerang's circular flight brings it back to the thrower.

A boomerang is held correctly when its curve points toward the thrower.

FACT:

SOME BOOMERANGS CAN HAVE THREE OR EVEN FOUR WINGS. MORE WINGS ALLOW THE BOOMERANG TO TURN IN TIGHTER CIRCLES.

lift—the force that lets something rise from the ground and stay in the air

STEALTHY SHURIKEN

Sometimes Batman uses Batarangs to smash windows, take out lights, and create distractions. In these cases, his Batarangs act more like Japanese throwing weapons called *shuriken*.

Shuriken date back hundreds of years to the time of samurai and ninja. These Japanese warriors were famous for their swords and fearsome fighting skills. But shuriken made excellent backup weapons. The shuriken's shallow points often weren't deadly. But they could easily catch an enemy off guard when thrown at their hands, feet, or face.

In the United States, shuriken are called throwing stars and ninja stars. But don't let these names fool you. Shuriken can have many different shapes. Historically, there were two basic designs: *bo shuriken* and *hira shuriken*.

Bo shuriken were straight, spike-like blades. They were often called "throwing needles." They had either one or two pointed ends. They worked like darts or arrows. Bo shuriken were thrown overhand like a baseball pitch.

Hira shuriken are more familiar to most people. These thin, star-shaped metal plates had sharpened blade tips. Unlike bo shuriken, hira shuriken had three to eight razor-sharp points. With a sharp flick of the wrist, hira shuriken were sent spinning through the air.

Modern-day ninja Jinichi Kawakami displays a collection of traditional Japanese weapons, including hira shuriken.

GRIPPING GRAPNELS

Sometimes Batman needs to rise above the concrete canyons of Gotham City. In these situations he fires his grapnel, or grappling hook, device. With a pull of the trigger, his grapnel and line help him scale skyscrapers.

The Romans invented grappling hooks more than 2,000 years ago. In naval battles, they threw dozens of grappling hooks to snag enemy ships. Then they'd pull the ships close enough for their soldiers to board.

Devices for firing grappling hooks exist today. But they're not nearly as small as Batman's. Digital Force Technologies has developed a tactical **pneumatic** launch system (T-PLS) for the U.S. Army. This system uses compressed air. It launches a titanium grappling hook and a Kevlar line 120 feet (37 meters) in the air.

But don't plan on adding a T-PLS to your own Utility Belt anytime soon. This launcher weighs 19 pounds (8.6 kilograms). It measures about 4 feet (1.2 m) long. The T-PLS also doesn't have a **winch** to pull you up the side of a building. You have to climb the rope yourself. Even so, the T-PLS is a handy military tool.

A soldier practices throwing a grappling hook during training.

ATLAS POWER ASCENDER

In 2005 a group of students at the Massachusetts Institute of Technology created a battery-powered rope **ascender**. The lightweight device, called the Atlas Power Ascender, is about the size of a power tool. It pulls a fully-geared soldier or firefighter up a rope at about 10 feet (3 m) per second.

pneumatic—operated by compressed air

winch—a machine that lifts or pulls heavy objects

ascender—a device used for climbing rope that slides freely in one direction and grips the rope when pulled in the other direction

CHAPTER 2

DISABLING THE ENEMY

Batman doesn't just fight crime—he stops it cold. With bolas, blowguns, and a tamper-proof Utility Belt, he stays one step ahead of his enemies.

THE BUSINESS OF BOLAS

If Batarangs don't knock villains off their feet, Batman's bolas trip them up. A bola is a throwing weapon made of weights connected with cords. Just like boomerangs, bolas were used as weapons and for hunting. They helped catch animals and birds by entangling their legs or wings. If thrown with enough force, bolas could even break bones.

Ancient hunters used bolas as effective weapons for catching prey.

Bolas date back thousands of years to the Stone Age. Over the centuries, the Inuit and the Chinese used them for hunting and warfare. South American gauchos, or cowboys, also used them to capture cattle by snaring their legs.

The bolas gauchos used had braided leather cords. The weights were usually wooden balls or small leather sacks filled with stones. Some bolas were works of art. They were made of ivory and covered with valuable metals.

Bolas had different names based on the number of weights. A *perdida* had one weight. A *boleadora* had three. Perdidas were usually used against people. Boleadoras were used for hunting wild cattle and large birds. Some bolas had up to eight weights.

BACKYARD BOLAS

Does anyone still use bolas today? Look no further than a game known as ladder ball, ladder toss, or lasso golf. This modern lawn game uses bolas. The game is played by throwing a two-ball bola onto a plastic ladder. Each ladder rung has a point value. The game's goal is to wrap the bolas around the rungs to score the most points.

OUT FOR THE COUNT

Batman doesn't use guns—at least ones that fire bullets. But he does have weapons to disable his enemies. For a quick knockout punch, he relies on his blowgun and **tranquilizer** darts.

In real life, tranquilizer darts aren't used on people. Instead, they're used for capturing wild animals. The darts are commonly fired from a tranquilizer gun or rifle. These weapons usually get their power from compressed gas cartridges. The burst of gas sends the tranquilizer-filled dart flying at the target.

tranquilizer—a drug that has a calming effect

paralyze—to cause a loss of the ability to control the muscles

The tranquilizers used in darts can be sedative, anesthetic, or paralytic drugs. Sedatives relax and calm an animal. Anesthetics knock them out. Paralytic drugs **paralyze** an animal's muscles so it can't move.

The drug dose needed to tranquilize an animal is based on its estimated weight. Heavier animals need a larger dose than smaller ones. But weight isn't the only deciding factor. Slowing down an excited elephant takes twice the dose as a calm elephant. And whenever an animal is darted, an antidote must be on hand. This drug reverses the tranquilizer's effect.

A veterinarian holds a tranquilizer dart used to sedate an elephant.

STUNNING SCIENCE

The amazing gadgets on Batman's Utility Belt get the most attention. But there's more to the belt itself than meets the eye. It is armed to stop criminals from tampering with it. These defenses don't cause permanent harm. But they do keep the Utility Belt from falling into the wrong hands.

Real-life duty belts aren't armed to stop people from taking them. But they do carry **nonlethal** weapons, such as Tasers, for controlling attackers. Tasers are electronic devices that can target someone from 20 feet (6 m) away. They allow officers to keep a safe distance while controlling a suspect.

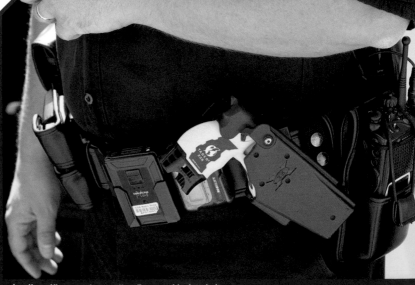

A police officer carries a yellow Taser on his duty belt.

nonlethal—not deadly

pulse—a steady beat or throb

nerve—a thin fiber that carries messages between the brain and other parts of the body

How does a Taser work? When the device is fired, two metal darts, or probes, fly at the target. The probes attach to the target and remain connected to the device with thin copper wires. Once the probes attach, they send electric **pulses** between each other. These pulses disrupt **nerve** communication between the muscles and the brain. The shock temporarily paralyzes the muscles. Most targets drop straight to the ground.

THE BODY ELECTRIC

Electronic control devices upset your body's electrical communication system. That's right, your body is electric! In fact, everything you do is controlled by electrical signals. Your body parts use small doses of electricity to communicate with each other. The electricity travels along your nerves and between your brain cells.

FACT:

A TASER'S PROBES DON'T NEED TO TOUCH SKIN. THEY'LL WORK EVEN IF THEY'RE SNAGGED IN CLOTHING.

17

CHAPTER 3

AN EXPLOSIVE ARSENAL

Sometimes Batman needs something with a bit more bang than a Batarang can deliver. From smoke bombs to flashbangs, the Caped Crusader has a variety of explosives. They help him control angry mobs, crash criminal hideouts, or make quick getaways.

DISAPPEARING ACT

Batman's skills make him a master of surprise. He often slips in and out of areas undetected. But even the Dark Knight sometimes needs help getting out of tight spots. Luckily, his Utility Belt carries smoke bombs to cover his escapes.

Smoke bombs are a type of firework. Instead of exploding with a shower of light, they produce huge clouds of smoke.

Many smoke bombs are walnut-sized hollow clay or cardboard balls filled with smoke-making chemicals. Some smoke bombs are lit directly. Others have a time-delayed ignition that uses a short fuse.

Either way, lighting the materials inside a smoke bomb causes a **chemical reaction**. The reaction produces gases and particles that combine to create a thick cloud of smoke. A typical smoke bomb releases smoke for about 10 to 15 seconds—just long enough to make a quick getaway.

Smoke bombs come in different sizes and shapes and can release all sorts of colors.

IGNITION ON IMPACT!

Batman's smoke bombs are sometimes ignited by impact rather than by lighting a fuse. In this case, the ignition source is a material used in Christmas crackers and bang snaps. The material is responsible for the loud "crack" you hear.

chemical reaction—process in which one or more substances change to form a new substance or substances

FLASH AND BANG

Sometimes Batman needs more than just smoke to distract his enemies. In these instances, he reaches for his flash grenades. Flash grenades are also known as stun grenades and flashbangs.

Flashbangs are nonlethal explosives that confuse an enemy's senses. When detonated, a chemical reaction creates a blinding flash of light. This extremely bright flash makes it impossible to see for about five seconds.

A soldier throws a flashbang during a training exercise.

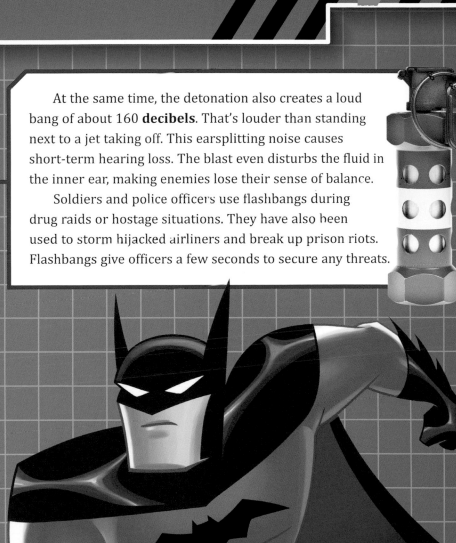

At the same time, the detonation also creates a loud bang of about 160 **decibels**. That's louder than standing next to a jet taking off. This earsplitting noise causes short-term hearing loss. The blast even disturbs the fluid in the inner ear, making enemies lose their sense of balance.

Soldiers and police officers use flashbangs during drug raids or hostage situations. They have also been used to storm hijacked airliners and break up prison riots. Flashbangs give officers a few seconds to secure any threats.

FACT:

DECIBELS ARE USED TO MEASURE SOUND INTENSITY. NORMAL BREATHING IS ABOUT 10 DECIBELS. A RUNNING VACUUM CLEANER IS ABOUT 70 DECIBELS. A JET ENGINE TAKING OFF IS 130 DECIBELS.

decibel—a unit for measuring the volume of sounds

BOMBS AWAY

Besides smoke bombs, Batman carries a variety of explosives on his Utility Belt. He uses them to blow up locks, destroy weapons, or disable villains' getaway cars. Many of his explosives are small bombs known as mini-grenades.

Grenades have been used in warfare for hundreds of years. Early grenades were just metal containers filled with gunpowder. Soldiers lit the wick and tossed the grenade before it could blow up in their hands.

Modern time-delayed grenades are far more sophisticated. The outer shell of the grenade is made of cast iron. It holds a chemical fuse, which is surrounded by explosive material. A spring-loaded striker triggers the grenade's firing mechanism. The striker is held in place by the striker lever. This lever is held in place by the safety pin.

Soldiers in the 12th Combat Aviation Brigade practice throwing hand grenades.

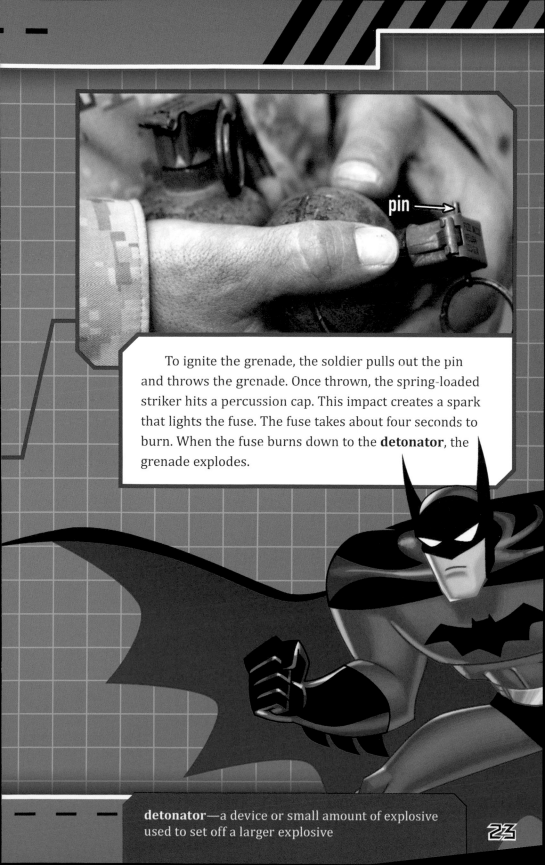

pin ⟶

To ignite the grenade, the soldier pulls out the pin and throws the grenade. Once thrown, the spring-loaded striker hits a percussion cap. This impact creates a spark that lights the fuse. The fuse takes about four seconds to burn. When the fuse burns down to the **detonator**, the grenade explodes.

detonator—a device or small amount of explosive used to set off a larger explosive

CHAPTER 4

PREPARED FOR ANYTHING

Batman must always be ready for anything—from studying crime scenes to traveling underwater. Luckily, his Utility Belt is loaded with more than just weapons. It always has the right tools for any task.

WATCHFUL EYES

Batman does much of his detective work from the shadows. He keeps a watchful eye on criminals without being seen himself. One tool that helps him see around and over walls is a periscope.

Periscopes use two mirrors to **reflect** light around corners. Light coming into the periscope bounces off a mirror set at a 45-degree angle. The reflected light travels down the periscope to a second mirror. This mirror sends the light to the user's eye.

Periscopes are very important for the military. Armored M1 Abrams tanks use periscopes to see the battlefield. Without leaving the tank, a commander uses several periscopes to see the entire surrounding area. Submarines also use periscopes. Sailors can see what's going on above the waves, even when the sub floats below them. In fact, a sub's periscope can be up to 60 feet (18 m) long.

A Marine using a hand-held periscope.

PHOTONICS MASTS

Periscopes on submarines may soon be a thing of the past. Photonics masts are replacing periscopes. They have digital equipment and sensors. A photonics mast rises above the water in a way similar to a car antenna. It holds **infrared** sensors and digital cameras. Images appear on display panels inside the sub.

FACT:

THE LONGER THE TUBE IN A PERISCOPE, THE SMALLER THE IMAGE LOOKS. PERISCOPES IN TANKS AND SUBMARINES HAVE MAGNIFYING LENSES BETWEEN THE MIRRORS. THEY MAKE THE REFLECTED IMAGE LARGER.

reflect—to bounce off an object

infrared—light waves in the electromagnetic spectrum between visible light and microwaves

CHECKING FOR PRINTS

As a superb detective, Batman has a keen eye for evidence villains leave behind. As a result, one of his most useful gadgets is his portable fingerprint analysis kit. It allows him to inspect fingerprints left at the scene of a crime.

Everyone has a unique pattern of ridges, valleys, and **whorls** on his or her fingertips. Police detectives study these patterns. If a person's fingerprints match those found at a crime scene, he or she could be a suspect.

For fingerprint identification, detectives look for visible and **latent** fingerprints. Visible prints are made on a surface that can hold an impression. Dirt and clay, for example, can sometimes hold prints that detectives can see.

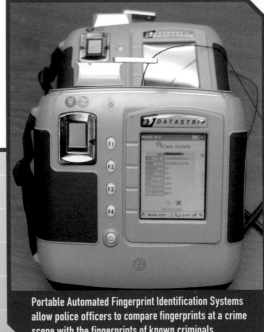

Portable Automated Fingerprint Identification Systems allow police officers to compare fingerprints at a crime scene with the fingerprints of known criminals.

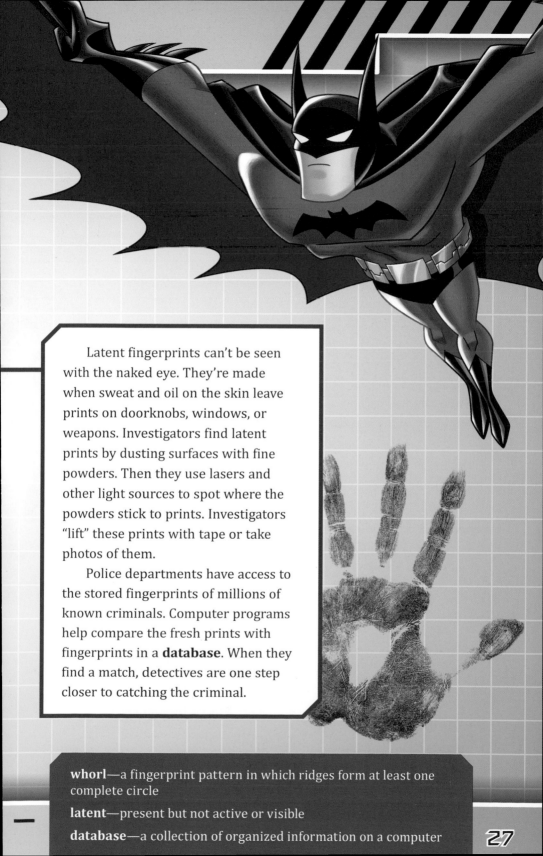

Latent fingerprints can't be seen with the naked eye. They're made when sweat and oil on the skin leave prints on doorknobs, windows, or weapons. Investigators find latent prints by dusting surfaces with fine powders. Then they use lasers and other light sources to spot where the powders stick to prints. Investigators "lift" these prints with tape or take photos of them.

Police departments have access to the stored fingerprints of millions of known criminals. Computer programs help compare the fresh prints with fingerprints in a **database**. When they find a match, detectives are one step closer to catching the criminal.

whorl—a fingerprint pattern in which ridges form at least one complete circle

latent—present but not active or visible

database—a collection of organized information on a computer

27

UNDERWATER DANGERS

Aquaman can breathe in the ocean's depths, but Batman needs a little help. For missions that take the Caped Crusader underwater, the rebreather on his Utility Belt helps him survive.

Advanced scuba divers and U.S. Navy SEALs also use rebreathers. These devices allow divers to breathe their own air over and over again. A chemical scrubber in the device removes carbon dioxide gas breathed out by the diver. Leftover oxygen and other gases are breathed in again.

Rebreathing air has its limits. As needed, the device also injects fresh oxygen from a small oxygen tank. It also controls the amount of oxygen being breathed in. Too much or too little oxygen can be dangerous.

A military diver uses a rebreather to move through the water.

Though expensive, rebreathers have some advantages over regular scuba equipment. They don't waste oxygen because they replace only what is used up. They also weigh less than normal scuba gear. Most importantly, rebreathers don't create bubbles. For military uses, rebreathers won't give away a diver's position to the enemy.

scuba gear

rebreather

A diver using a rebreather doesn't release air bubbles like a diver using scuba gear.

UTILITY FOR THE FUTURE

From Batarangs to rebreathers, Batman has an endless supply of gadgets. Just when you think you've seen everything, the Caped Crusader uses a tool you weren't expecting. While many of these devices seem fictional, most have real-world connections. What tools will the Dark Knight use in the future? No one knows for sure. But advancements in real-world science and engineering will likely find a place on Batman's Utility Belt.

GLOSSARY

ascender (uh-SEND-uhr)—a device used for climbing rope that slides freely in one direction and grips the rope when pulled in the other direction

chemical reaction (KE-muh-kuhl ree-AK-shuhn)—process in which one or more substances change to form a new substance or substances

database (DAY-tuh-bays)—a collection of organized information on a computer

decibel (DE-suh-buhl)—a unit for measuring the volume of sounds

detonator (DET-uh-nate-uhr)—a device or small amount of explosive used to set off a larger explosive

infrared (in-fruh-RED)—light waves in the electromagnetic spectrum between visible light and microwaves

latent (LAY-tuhnt)—present but not active or visible

lift (LIFT)—the force that lets something rise from the ground and stay in the air

nerve (NURV)—a thin fiber that carries messages between the brain and other parts of the body

nonlethal (NON-lee-thul)—not deadly

paralyze (PA-ruh-lize)—to cause a loss of the ability to control the muscles

pneumatic (noo-MAT-ik)—operated by compressed air

pulse (PUHLSS)—a steady beat or throb

reflect (ri-FLEKT)—to bounce off an object

tranquilizer (TRANG-kwul-lye-zur)—a drug that has a calming effect

whorl (HWOR-uhl)—a fingerprint pattern in which ridges form at least one complete circle

winch (WINCH)—a machine that lifts or pulls heavy objects

READ MORE

Blackford, Cheryl. *This Book Is Top Secret: A Collection of Awesome Military Trivia.* Super Trivia Collection. North Mankato, Minn.: Capstone Press, 2013.

Dougherty, Martin J. *Weapons and Technology.* Modern Warfare. Pleasantville, N.Y.: GS Learning Library, 2010.

Labrecque, Ellen. *Fighting Crime.* Heroic Jobs. Chicago: Raintree, 2012.

Snedden, Robert. *Crime-Fighting Devices.* Sci-Hi: Science and Technology. Chicago: Raintree, 2011.

INTERNET SITES

FactHound offers a safe, fun way to find Internet sites related to this book. All of the sites on FactHound have been researched by our staff.

Here's all you do:

Visit **www.facthound.com**

Type in this code: 9781476539430

INDEX